HIDDEN & HAU
UNDERGROUND
EDINBURGH

ALAN J WILSON, DES BROGAN,
FRANCES HOLLINRAKE

The most complete history of Edinburgh's world-famous
Mary King's Close and the newly discovered
Underground Vaults of the South Bridge

A Mercat Tours of Edinburgh Publication

First Published 1999
© Mercat Tours of Edinburgh, 1999

Published by Mercat Tours
Mercat House
Niddry Street South
Edinburgh EH1 1NS
Scotland

info@mercat-tours.co.uk

A CIP catalogue record for this book is available from
the British Library

ISBN 0 9536198 0 X

Acknowledgements

All photographs by Andrew Hollinrake. Cover photograph by
Jonathan Cosens Photography.
Prints from Grant's *Old and New Edinburgh*. Mary King's Close
Testament [p5] used with kind permission of the National Archives of
Scotland, cc8/8/61f86r. Frontispiece of *Satan's Invisible World
Discovered* [p10] used courtesy of Edinburgh City Libraries. Carved
stone panel photograph [p15] used by kind permission of the National
Museums of Scotland 1999.

Printed by Geo. Stewart & Co Ltd, Edinburgh

Underground Edinburgh

There can be few people in Edinburgh who have not heard of the city's legendary 'Underground City'. Many are the tales of secret tunnels, dark passageways and whole streets perfectly preserved, complete with curtains on the windows and bread still lying, fossilised by age, in ancient shop windows. There has been a growing interest in these hidden parts of Edinburgh – an interest that has led to archaeological excavation, research and greater knowledge. The discoveries made, however, are quite different from the 'Underground City' of popular imagination. While there is no great labyrinth of streets beneath our city, there are indeed several underground locations, long hidden from public view. Some of these have been in constant use for centuries. Some have only been opened to the public in the last few years. Not only are the tales that are told in this book from the distant past, they come also from more recent times. Many visitors have experienced unexplained phenomena. Haunted or not, Edinburgh's hidden underground continues to fascinate and frighten visitors and local people alike. Within these pages the true history is told, accompanied by tales of past and present, to satisfy curiosity, to allow a glimpse into another world and to send a shiver down the spine of the most sceptical.

Underground Edinburgh awaits.

MARY KING'S CLOSE

The Early History

The historic Royal Mile forms the backbone of the old city of Edinburgh. It is full of wonderful old closes and hidden courtyards dating back centuries. However, the most famous close in the Royal Mile is hidden from view, accessible only by arrangement. Buried beneath an 18th century quadrangle in the High Street lie the remains of Mary King's Close, reputed to be the most haunted place in Edinburgh.

There can be no doubt that the legends of Mary King's Close have spread far and wide. This hidden, underground street has fascinated people for centuries and many tales have been told of the tragic plague victims and their tortured spirits. Mary King's Close is a place where history and mystery exist side by side.

To uncover the secrets of the ancient street we must go back to Edinburgh in the 16th century when it was a busy bustling capital built upon the ridge of an ancient volcanic rock. The Royal Mile, stretching from Edinburgh Castle to the Palace of Holyroodhouse, forms the centre of the city. Sixteenth century residents would recognise the heart of the city today. The High Kirk of St. Giles dominates the High Street and the Mercat Cross is still a place of Royal Proclamations and meetings of the townsfolk. The Tolbooth no longer stands, although there is a stone heart set into the cobblestones to mark its place. On the opposite side of the road stands a building that no 16th

Mary King's Close today

2

The heart of the Old Town

century observer would recognise. The City Chambers, a large quadrangle, with imposing arches around a spacious courtyard, was not constructed until 1753. In 1500 on this side of the street stood a collection of closes, the narrow alleyways that slope steeply away on either side of the Royal Mile.

Today the closes of the Old Town have their names clearly displayed, often accompanied by a plaque recalling important characters or events. In the sixteenth century there were no such street signs, and the closes would often be named after their most important resident. But the names often changed with the passing of the years. The street that would eventually become Mary King's Close was known by several names – Brown's Close, Livingstone's Close and Touris Close, the latter after a prominent land-owning family. George Touris was a Lord Provost of the city and his name can still be seen on the plaque of former Lord Provosts within the City Chambers.

At the beginning of the 17th century, the street was known as Alexander King's Close. Alexander was originally from Dryden, but worked as a lawyer in Edinburgh from 1580 until his death in 1619. He was successful, powerful and wealthy in his professional field, but privately he was a deeply unpopular man. The Edinburgh folk would whisper dark tales of witchcraft, telling one another that Mr. King was in league with the Devil himself. The townsfolk would walk cautiously down the street, peering in at the windows, half-expecting to see satanic rituals being performed before their very

eyes! What could have inspired such suspicion? Was it simply envy of a successful, rich man? Most likely it was because Alexander King was a Roman Catholic and since the Reformation in 1560 Scotland had been a Protestant country. Catholics were treated with caution and suspicion and if a Catholic like Mr King could rise to such prominence many townsfolk believed it was with the help of the Devil. By 1620, Alexander King's Close already had a sinister reputation in the town that would grow with each passing century.

Alexander King, as far as we know, had no children. His heir was his brother, Adam, who did not take up residency in the street although an area of wasteland is listed in 1635 as being *The property of Alexander King or his heirs.*

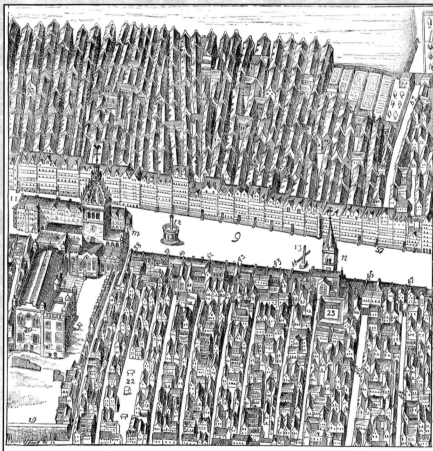

PLAN OF EDINBURGH, FROM ST. GILES'S TO HACKERSTON'S WYND. *(After Gordon of Rothiemay.)*

9, The High Street ; 11, The Tolbooth ; 12, The High Cross or Market Cross ; 13, The Tron ; 19, Meal Market ; 20, The Parliament House ; 22, The Fish Market ; 23, The Flesh Market ; 38, S. Monan's Wynd ; 39, Fish Market Wynd ; 40, Borthwick's Wynd ; 41, Conn's Close ; 42, Bell's Wynd ; 43, Steven Law's Close ; 44, Peebles Wynd ; 45, Marlin's Wynd ; 46, Niddry's Wynd ; 47, Dickson's Close ; 48, The Blackfriars Wynd ; 57, Hackerston's Wynd ; *m*, The Great Kirk, or St. Giles's Kirk ; *n*, The Tron Kirk.

Old Closes of the Royal Mile

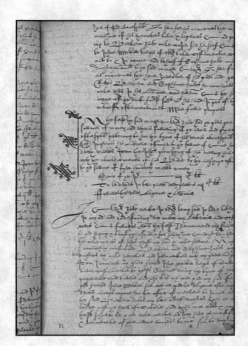

Mary King's Testament

Alexander now leaves our story, as we turn our attention to a new resident in the street, one Mary King. In the tax records of 1635 Mary is listed as living near the top of the street on the west side. She rented a house from J. Bannentyne, described as a *turnpike house.... with a cellar*. By the time she moved into the street Mary King was already a widow. Her husband, Thomas Nimmo, had been a merchant Burgess in the city, a position that allowed him certain trading privileges and the right to carry a musket. Married in 1616 in Edinburgh, Mary bore her husband three children – Euphame, Janet and William, before Thomas died in 1629. It is likely that on her husband's death, Mary moved into Alexander King's Close (also known as King's Close). Within a few short years the street had taken her name and retained it after her own demise in 1644. We are very fortunate in that Mary left us clues about herself which give us a vivid insight into early 17th century life.

The Nor' Loch

The Scottish Records Office in Edinburgh holds a document listing the possessions Mary owned before she died. It would appear Mary liked her comforts. She owned many soft furnishings such as cushions, bolsters and pillows. Her home was well supplied with cooking pans and utensils including two chamber pots. Bolts of cloth and spools of thread were found amongst Mary's possessions, so perhaps she took up sewing to keep herself busy or to provide a small income. Perhaps on a cold winter's night as she sat sewing by the fire, Mary would have a wee dram to keep out the chill. For Mary King, respectable elderly widow, had a very well stocked cellar containing wine, whisky and several barrels of beer. Was Mary a good and amiable hostess furnishing her guests with samples from her cellar?

In the early 17th century, when Mary King was still living, her street was the largest of the closes on the north side of the High Street. City records show us that there were entrances to the houses on both sides of the close, something of a

A laigh house in Mary King's Close

rarity at the time as most closes only had entrances on one side. Mary King's Close also seems to be the only one of the group that ran the full length of the sloping hillside, right to the shores of the Nor' Loch. This loch (now Princes Street Gardens) was the result of a natural valley that was dammed in the 16th century to defend against English attack. It would certainly have provided a powerful deterrent for any invading army. The Nor' Loch, far from being a tranquil pool for recreation and pastoral meditation, was a foul and stinking thing. It served as a rubbish dump for Edinburgh, where the market debris, household waste and raw sewage of the city would be flung day after day. In later years, it was discovered to be the resting-place of hundreds of dead bodies. No wonder that the more wealthy inhabitants of Mary King's Close chose to live at the top of the street rather than at the bottom.

Until the late 18th century, when the New Town was conceived and built, there was little social division in Edinburgh. Often, rich and poor would live together in one street in a rather higgledy-piggledy fashion, sharing the same small front door and narrow turnpike stair. Within one tenement though, the difference in social class was apparent; the lower sections of society would live on street level close to the squalor of the filthy alleyways, or on the highest levels, which were apt to shake in high winds. The wealthier classes meanwhile, would occupy the middle floors and avoid the hazards above and below them. In a street such as Mary King's Close it was not at all unusual to find a variety of properties, from one-roomed *laigh* houses to homes with several floors, windows and staircases.

The Pestilence

In the mid-17th century Edinburgh was a very overcrowded city. The city wall, built to keep out invaders, had also served to keep the citizens within. As the population of Edinburgh grew, the city did not expand outwards (as was to happen in the 18th century), it expanded upwards. Tenements that seemed to touch the sky crowded together in the narrow city streets and the closes were often dark, damp, slippery places with little sunlight. It is believed that the highest building that existed in Mary King's Close was eleven storeys high. In a cramped and dirty city that had little or no sanitation, disease would often take its toll. Edinburgh was no exception. In 1645, the

city of Edinburgh was devastated by an outbreak of the plague – an epidemic that would have tragic and far-reaching con-sequences.

In 1644, before Mary King had died, terrible warnings of the plague began to reach Edinburgh from the continent. The officials at the Port of Leith were instructed to check every ship that came into harbour for signs of the illness. Unfortunately, such

Inside Mary King's Close

precautionary measures were made in vain. By the spring of 1645 the disease had spread to many parts of the city and it was clear to the council that this would be a long and bitter epidemic.

Rattus Rattus

With the benefit of hindsight, we can trace the outbreak of the plague to *Rattus Rattus*, more commonly known as the black or ship's rat. The rats carried the fleas on their furry bodies that transmitted the bacteria to the human population. If the sufferer contracted bubonic plague, the first symptom was often a bad cold, followed by horrible swellings in the armpit, neck or groin. Filled with evil-smelling mucous, these boils or *buboes* would burst, causing unbearable agony. If the victims were reasonably strong and healthy they could survive though greatly weakened. The pneumonic plague, however, was fatal in all cases. As well as causing the symptoms of the bubonic plague, the pneumonic form attacked the lungs and caused massive haemorrhaging throughout the body. Death was mercifully quick – only a day in some cases.

In 1645, little was known about contagion or the spread of disease. Many things were blamed for this terrifying outbreak. Did the soldiers of English armies bring it to Scotland? Was it a blow dealt by God as a punishment for wickedness? Was the disease the work of the Devil and his servants? Would it only stop when everybody in the city was dead? There was much discontent in Edinburgh about the political regime and the reign of Charles I. One poet, William Drummond, summed it up in a succinct verse:

> *Turne, citizens, to God; repent, repent,*
> *And praye your bedlam frenzies may relent:*
> *Think not rebellion a trifling thing –*
> *This plague doth fight for Mary and the King!*

Some Edinburgh residents decided to leave the city before it was too late. Many wealthy families escaped to estates in the country or to relatives in parts of Scotland that were less affected. The University took the decision to abandon the graduation ceremonies for that year and sent all the students away. In the summer of 1645 the city gates were closed; nobody could enter Edinburgh and nobody could leave. Those that were left inside the city tried any measures they could to prevent the worst. Burning fierce fires night and day seemed to increase the chances of survival. While the people of Edinburgh did not know that the heat was killing the fleas that carried the disease, they just knew that it worked. The doctors of the

Bruntsfield Links

city worked around the clock dressed in special clothing to protect themselves. They carried dried herbs and flowers to ward off evil and tried to soothe fevers and fears by giving gin to their patients. Huge boiling vats were set up in the open spaces to clean the clothes and belongings of infected families. But of all the professions in Edinburgh that year, the busiest by far were the church ministers and the gravediggers.

Mary King's Close and nearby streets were badly affected by the plague as this was one of the most overcrowded and rat-infested parts of the city. The inhabitants lived in a cramped and dirty street and the infection spread quickly in such conditions. The people of Edinburgh, however, still had their suspicions about the close and its Catholic associations. They believed that God was punishing those within for their sins and they had little pity for the residents of Mary King's Close. The burgh records of the plague epidemic speak of buildings and streets that were *steekit* or closed up although they rarely mention the exact location. Though difficult to verify, local tradition has it that Mary King's Close and the surrounding streets were effectively quarantined. Whatever the horrific details, it is certain that many hundreds of people died there, in fear and in squalor. The graveyards of Edinburgh were unable to cope with the vast numbers of dead, so mass graves were opened up in various quarters, including the Meadows, Leith Links and Holyrood Park. The victims of Mary King's Close are believed to be buried under Bruntsfield Links. Without ceremony, coffins or marker of remembrance.

The plague raged for over a year in the city of Edinburgh, resulting in the deaths of nearly half the population. The Town Council Records state that the cost to the city *for time of pestilence* was £10,792 6s 8d. It was by far the worst outbreak of the plague in the city's history.

The haunted legend

Many people today like to imagine, with a shudder, that Mary King's Close was abandoned forever following the plague epidemic. They picture the abandoned streets left as they were in 1645 with the only inhabitants being the ghosts of the hapless victims. This, however, is far from the truth. Edinburgh in the late 17th century was still an overcrowded city with property much sought after. Gruesome though it may seem to us, the houses within Mary King's Close and the other streets were occupied once again by the end of the 1600s. This is not to say, of course, that there were no mentions of the spirits.

In 1685 a remarkable book was published which was to seal the ghostly reputation of Mary King's Close once and for all. It was

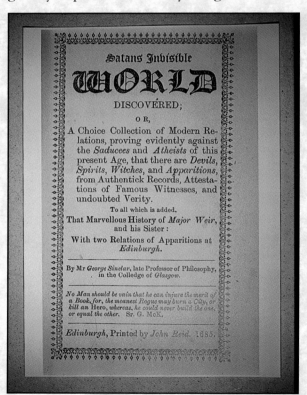

written by Professor George Sinclair of Glasgow University and was entitled *Satan's Invisible World Discovered.* The frontispiece promises us nothing less than *A choice collection, proving evidently that there are devils, spirits, witches and apparitions, from authentic records and attestations of famous witness....* Within its leather-bound covers can be found many of the most famous supernatural Edinburgh tales; the evil wizard of the

Frontispiece to Satan's Invisible World

West Bow, Thomas Weir, the devil-worshipping witches burned for their sins and of course, the ghostly apparitions of Mary King's Close. An honest lawyer, Thomas Coltheart, and his wife were beset one night by all manner of spirits and tortured souls. We read of disembodied heads, of strange malformed ghostly animals, of thin miserable children and of the spectral arm that seemed insistent on shaking Mr. Coltheart by the hand. It would seem that everybody's suspicions about the street were true and it was indeed haunted by the tragic plague victims.

This extraordinary book, however, was written with a purpose. The author, George Sinclair, was a man of scientific knowledge who had published several academic papers on the properties of coal gas and 'hydrostaticks'. Did he himself believe that the street was haunted? Or would he have concluded that the foetid Nor' Loch produced hazy gas clouds that lingered in the dark, dingy streets, frightening the inhabitants? Whatever his own personal feelings, Professor Sinclair wrote the book in order to scare people. He was a very religious man, watchful for any sign of the devil and his works. The citizens of Edinburgh, he thought, needed to be brought closer to God and they needed to be frightened into being more Godly. *Satan's Invisible World* was a book of religious propaganda, published at a time of great fear and superstition, when people believed in witchcraft and demonology. The book contained an irresistible combination of scaremongering, moral outrage and gruesome detail that would make any modern tabloid editor happy. As an accurate historic document, *Satan's Invisible World* should be treated with caution. It is a fine example of how legends are made; legends that have lasted for over three hundred years and show no signs of being forgotten.

At the turn of the 18th century, with the tales of horror still in their minds, the people of Edinburgh were not at all surprised when a number of fires broke out on the north side of the High Street. God, apparently, had not finished with Mary King's Close. One account of the time tells how He shot *three lamentable fiery darts...to stir up and awake the inhabitants thereof from impietie."* In 1702, after the third fire had raged, a schoolmaster, James Porterfield warned,

> *Therefore be pious, and go sin no more,*
> *Nor cherish sins, as ye have done before,*
> *For God, for sins, hath many plagues in store*

Some of the properties at the top of Mary King's Close suffered considerable damage, but the rest of the street continued to attract shops and businesses as before. By 1750 there were nearly thirty

The Royal Exchange and Coffee House

families living in the street and a wide variety of businesses. We find merchants, a wigmaker, glovers, a tavern and an ale seller with the rather unfortunate name of John Skeleton. A large eight-storey tenement at the head of the close was home to the Edinburgh Fishmonger's Company Oyster Bar, open until 10pm, selling fresh and pickled oysters. The stories of the grisly past may have been told with relish, but life went on in Mary King's Close nonetheless.

Steps and window of the Coffee House

Later Developments

Edinburgh in the late 18th century was an exciting place. Great advances were made throughout Europe in science, art and philosophy. Edinburgh was at the forefront of new thought and ideas, home as it was to David Hume, James Hutton and Robert Adam. In keeping with the modern, enlightened times, the city council decided to construct a new building on the High Street in 1752. The neo-classical quadrangle was to include a merchants' trading hall and certain chambers for holders of civic office. The committee that was appointed to draw up the proposals noted that this would be a fine opportunity to remove older streets that had fallen into disrepair. They wrote that *several of the principal parts of the town are now lying in ruins. Many of the old houses are decaying.* Mary King's Close is mentioned as *a disreputable quarter where the last dregs of the plague secreted themselves and the place was believed by the populace to be haunted.*

The land bought for the new building included Mary King's Close, Stewart's Close, Pearson's Close, and Allan's Close. Parts of these ancient closes were removed and what remained was to serve as the foundations for the new building. With great ceremony, the foundation stone for the Royal Exchange was laid on 13 September 1753. The inscription on the stone was carved in Latin and tells of *an innumerable multitude, all applauding.* Another nine months passed before building began, but the Royal Exchange was completed in 1761 at a cost to the city of £31,500.

Mary King's Close was not, as popular talk would have it, completely swallowed up by the Royal Exchange. Only the top part of the street

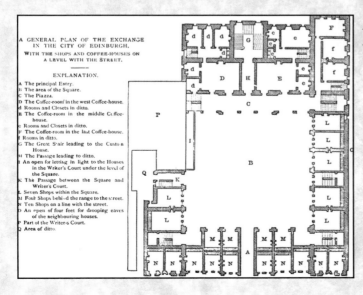

Plans of the Royal Exchange

became covered over. The eight-storey tenement continued to stand as part of the courtyard with staircases built to allow access to the street. (One of these is still visible today). The old houses were given vaulted ceilings to support the weight of the building and a new staircase was constructed to give direct access from the Royal Exchange to the street underneath. A section of an old tenement became the Royal Exchange Coffee House, where many of the lawyers of Edinburgh would partake of fine claret before their court business. The entrance was reached from the courtyard directly above. Part of the stone steps can still be seen jutting out from the wall.

The Coffee House was home to the infamous Wig Club, an organisation whose ceremonies focussed on a wig that was said to endow the wearer with great potency. The wig had a long illustrious history. It was reputed to have been given by the Queen of Sheba to King Solomon, then passed from Cleopatra to Mark Anthony (to hide an unfortunate bald spot). It made its way to Scotland in the luggage of none other than Bonnie Prince Charlie. The club boasted many strange and rude artefacts although it did not boast great philosophical debate!

The building of the Royal Exchange did not lessen activity in the streets partially buried within. Many parts of Mary King's Close were given new addresses as part of the Royal Exchange, Writer's Court and Market Street. This actually increased trade with businesses catering for the Royal Exchange being particularly successful, along with vintners and printers workshops. For several decades the name of Mary King's Close faded into memory. Had people finally forgotten the horrors of the past?

Cockburn Street

In 1856, interest was renewed in the close

Carved stone panel found in Mary King's Close

and its past, when work began on a new thoroughfare, Cockburn Street. This steep, curving road was to link the old and new parts of the town and cut a swathe through the closes descending from the Royal Mile. The lower section of Mary King's Close was completely demolished, so all that remained was the section underneath the Royal Exchange, now known as the City Chambers. A staircase was built from the close to Cockburn Street to allow access and was only removed in 1913. Those who believe that Mary King's Close is a recent discovery are mistaken. As late as the 1960s there were still people in Edinburgh who remembered shopping there!

During the construction of Cockburn Street, an unexpected treasure was unearthed. Lying face down in the cellar of one of the houses was a carved stone panel, depicting a touching scene. We can see a man on his deathbed (beneath which is a chamber pot), receiving last rites from a priest. His little children weep at his bedside as the last sacrament is given. The panel is believed to be part of an altar retable dating from the 15th century and it is probable that it was hidden during the Reformation, a time when many Catholic icons were destroyed. The panel is on display at the Museum of Scotland in Edinburgh and is one of the few surviving artefacts of the ancient Mary King's Close.

Sawmakers workshop and storeroom

The section of street that remained after Cockburn Street was built received a number of improvements, such as an iron handrail and a stone gutter. A few businesses continued to operate for a while, but the council was keen to close up Mary King's Close for good and use it for their own purposes. One of the last businesses to operate was that of the Chesneys, a family of sawmakers. One of the oldest rooms of the street became their workshop. The stairs leading down into the room are from the 17th century and the chimney breast can be seen on the left-hand wall. This was an old *laigh* house, home to a poor family in centuries past.

Embedded in the ceiling are a number of iron hooks, which have led many to believe that the room was once a butcher's shop. There is little evidence to support this and the hooks were probably put up by the Chesneys to hang their wares. This, in turn, has led to lurid speculation about the reddish-brown substance on the walls. Taken by many to be blood, it is in fact the pipes behind the walls that have rusted over the years and resulted in such sinister-looking stains.

The last owner of the room, Andrew Chesney, also lived in Mary King's Close. His house can be seen further down the slope from the workshop and may be entered through a big wooden front door. The interior of this house dates from about 1750, although there is little to see. The 19th century sanitary arrangements are quite impressive. A wooden thunderbox, or earth closet, remains waiting in the gloom. Mr. Chesney sold most of his property to the council in 1891 and moved out in 1893. His house was occupied by William Marshall, another sawmaker, from 1893-7, although he did not carry out his trade here. By the beginning of the 20th century, all trace of activity and occupation were gone from Mary King's Close. In the remains of the other streets buried beneath the City Chambers, the council provided offices for public officials and storage for the city records.

In the early years of the 20th century it seemed as if Mary King's Close had come to the end of its useful life. And yet the old street was pressed into service once more during the years of the Second World War. When conflict broke out, the government set in place a nation-wide air raid protection scheme to provide shelter for the population against attack from above. Local Authority inspectors searched Edinburgh for suitable locations and found them in the form of cellars, vaults and old railway tunnels. The remains of the old streets beneath the City Chambers were converted into shelters. This meant that many of the rooms were whitewashed and the ceilings were given a coat of concrete to act as reinforcement. Remnants of wartime can still be seen in the close, such as the No Smoking signs and the numbers pinned up above the doors.

The council personnel used the rooms during air raids, and much of the city's finest glass and china were stored in Mary King's Close.

Air Raid shelters in Mary King's Close

GHOSTLY TALES of MARY KING'S CLOSE

Most Edinburgh folk know at least one ghost story about Mary King's Close and as is the case with such stories, many have assumed mythical proportions. Here are just a few of the strange tales that have emerged in recent times.

The Lady in Black

There have been various sightings in the close of a tall woman, dressed in a long black or brown dress. She seems to wander freely about Mary King's Close and beyond. Several council staff members have reported that she haunts the City Chambers. One employee describes how he was working late one night and saw a tall, dark figure walk past his door. He called out, then went to the door and looked down the corridor and glimpsed a shadow passing into the room next door. He went in to investigate, fearing intruders, but there was nobody at all to be found. On another occasion, whilst in Mary King's Close, another Council employee saw the dark shadow of a woman walking past a doorway further up the street. When he ran after her, he found, with a shiver, that the close was completely deserted. Some have suggested that she is none other than the ghost of Mary King herself while others have argued that she is a spirit from a later period, possibly the Victorian era. A guide who frequently gives guided tours around the close (and regularly experiences strange phenomena) has described her as a 19th century spirit, probably middle-aged, who walks with a very straight back and wears the sombre, high-necked gowns of her time.

Mary King's Close today

The Worried Man

On several separate occasions, visitors to the close have sighted a short gentleman in a vaguely agitated state walking up the street. A group of visitors to the close were taking a guided tour round Mary King's Close, and at one point stood by the wooden door that led into the Chesneys' house. One lady later told the guide that she had seen a man aged between 55-60, walking down the corridor to the open door. She described him as short and somewhat dishevelled. She also said that he seemed very preoccupied with something, as if he had just received some bad news. On one unforgettable occasion, a guide was walking out of a house in Mary King's Close and felt a hand shoot out from the wall and grab his arm! A visitor on the tour said he looked terrified and she could verify that there was nobody near him at the time. Could this have been the ghost of Mr. Chesney or Mr. Marshall? Or was it a spectre from an earlier age?

The Noises from Above

This is a story told and verified by a council employee concerning a group of people who spent the night in Mary King's Close to raise money for charity. Whilst most people would shudder at such an idea, these fearless souls braved the underground streets to fundraise for a local hospital. Assembled in one room, they settled down to what they hoped would be a peaceful night. They hardly slept a wink! The council was apparently holding a reception in the rooms above. The sounds of glasses chinking, laughter and general merriment made it impossible to sleep. In the morning the participants mentioned this to the Chambers staff and wondered why they had not been warned about the party. They were met with blank looks – what party? There had been no event the previous evening. Even if there were, it would have been impossible to hear the noise several floors below. So what could explain such a thing? It has been suggested that the room in which they spent the night was once an old tavern. The room is certainly a strange shape for a house, long and cavernous. Perhaps another explanation is that the room above was once part of the Royal Exchange Coffee House where the advocates and lawyers of the 18th century would gather to drink and discuss their cases. Whatever the cause, the fundraisers swore that they would never return. What do you think?

The Little Girl

The story of the young girl is probably the most famous story about Mary King's Close although the house in which she has been seen is

actually part of another street, Allan's Close. This particular area is one of the best-preserved parts of the old streets beneath the City Chambers. A short corridor, once part of Pearson's Close, leads down a small flight of steps through an opening in the wall. This doorway would not have existed before 1753 and the entrance to the property was on the other side of the rooms on Allan's Close. The wall has been knocked through and here it is possible to see the thickness of the walls which are over 1.5 metres wide. The interior walls boast some charming decoration in the form of stencilled flowers. In one small room there is a wooden floor, a stone fireplace and a bricked up window, which once looked out onto Allan's Close. It was beneath this window that the little ghost was seen.

A television company from Japan came to Britain with a psychic and planned to film her in various places that were reputed to be haunted, recording any reaction that she had. The lady was brought to Edinburgh and taken to Mary King's Close although she was not told the story of the plague. On entering this area, the lady felt the presence of many people huddled miserably under blankets. She stepped into the small room but stepped back again saying that

Gifts left for the little girl ghost

there was too much unhappiness and that she did not want to go into the room. As she turned away, she felt a sharp tugging on the back of her trouser leg and when she walked back into the room there was the figure of a young girl standing beneath the window. The child was wearing ragged clothes and had dirty long hair. She was crying. When the psychic questioned this little ghost, she found that the child had died of 'the

The stone staircase

sickness' in 1645. She was terribly upset about losing her doll and felt very lonely. The psychic was moved to tears by this story and revealed that in her culture, it was considered very bad luck for the spirits of the past to be unhappy or restless. To ensure peace in the afterlife, gifts are offered. One of the cameramen attached to the film team was sent out into the Royal Mile to purchase such a gift. He bought her a doll, which was then placed beneath the window. It remains there to this day, surrounded by many more dolls, soft toys, sweets and gifts that have been left for her.

Whether the stories are true or not, the room with the toys is a strange place. Visitors from all over the world have made their way to the City Chambers in order to leave her a gift. More than any of the other ghosts reputed to haunt these ancient streets, the spirit of the little girl seems to encapsulate the terrible tragedy of the plague epidemic. Her story has moved people greatly and her fame has spread far and wide. We can only hope that the hundreds of gifts have made her a little happier.

The Staircase

In 1753, when the Royal Exchange was built, various alterations were made to the old streets to make them more accessible. In some cases this meant knocking through walls or reinforcing ceilings to support the weight of the building above. At this time a large stone staircase

was built to link the old streets internally. The space beneath this staircase housed stock belonging to Mr. Walker, a bookseller. Many of the business records of Mr. Walker have survived, listing clients (including the parents of Walter Scott) and detailing orders for periodicals and journals of the day.

Although dating from the 18th century, this staircase has been the location of several unexplained sightings. Several people have felt great unease at walking down the steps, saying that they felt they were being watched. A tour guide working in the close has sensed the presence of an unfriendly man glaring at the people on the tour. On another occasion, a tour guide caught a fleeting glimpse of a man in a dark blue cloak walking quickly up the staircase away from the group. Who this man might be, or why he is so hostile is a mystery. What is certain is that this is an area of Mary King's Close that makes people feel very uncomfortable.

Strange Currents

Several of the rooms in Mary King's Close have experienced unexplained electrical disturbances. A section of rooms once used for storing legal records have been known to cause alarm for the staff working there. An electric fire switches itself on and off, despite the area being securely locked and lights often fuse for no reason. On one memorable occasion, a group of workmen in Mary King's Close were sitting down for a well-earned tea break. The quiet was shattered by an electric drill suddenly springing to life, despite the fact that nobody was near it at the time. The workmen were extremely alarmed and found they could not switch off the drill without endangering themselves. Eventually, in a shower of sparks, the drill fell lifeless to the floor and would not work again. A freak power surge was the official explanation given for this incident but the workmen speculated that perhaps the ghosts simply wanted a bit of peace and quiet! The tour guides who conduct visitors around the close have often complained of light bulbs flickering or going out all together, plunging the group into darkness. This special effect is not guaranteed on all the tours!

Despite pestilence, fire and war, Mary King's Close has survived in some form or other for nearly five hundred years. What remains will hopefully be preserved for future generations. As long as people want to hear them, Mary King's Close still has its tales to tell.

THE VAULTS BENEATH THE
SOUTH BRIDGE

The South Bridge, spanning the Cowgate and linking the Royal Mile with Edinburgh's Southside, has stood for over 200 years. A monumental feat of engineering skill, it was considered a wonder in its day and gave Edinburgh its first purpose-built shopping area. Beneath the shops and the road stand the nineteen enormous stone arches that support the bridge. Although not visible from the outside, the arches hide an extensive honeycomb of vaulted rooms, dark passages and damp underground chambers that have only recently been discovered. This area of Edinburgh has many strange tales to tell.

The Construction of South Bridge

While the South Bridge was part of an extensive Edinburgh improvement scheme, it resulted in the destruction of some of the

The vaults today

city's older buildings and streets. A few fragments of this ancient past still remain but most of the medieval buildings were demolished and their stone used for the construction of the bridge. The stories of those past times are still with us and form part of Edinburgh's rich heritage.

One of the casualties of the South Bridge construction was the medieval Niddry's Wynd, with its picturesque but rather insanitary mansions. The name Niddry was one of

the oldest in Edinburgh having come to Scotland with Queen Margaret wife of Malcolm III in the 11th century. The family is mentioned in the royal charters of David II and Robert III, and the earliest mention of a street bearing the name came in 1477.

Niddry's Wynd appears many times in the city records; the street appears to have been home to some important characters and witness to several startling events. King James VI had friends

George Lockhart, resident of Niddry's Wynd

here with whom he would often dine before proceeding in State to Parliament. The King even lodged in the wynd for a time at the house of Nicol Edward, the Dean of Guild and sometime Lord Provost. It was not at all unusual for monarchs to use their friends' houses in this way. Lack of space and money was a problem for the Scottish crown and the private houses of richer individuals were often requisitioned for royal use.

Provost Edward's house was quite new when James VI lodged there. An older building had been destroyed in 1571 by the forces of Mary Queen of Scots during the civil war. It was, we are told, *distroyit be reasson of the inlaik of fyre*. The Provost's new house was built around a courtyard entered by a deep archway. The mansion contained thirteen rooms and included *a profound dungeon which was only accessible by a secret trap door*. Here King James and his Queen, Anne stayed after their return from Denmark and also James took refuge in the house in 1591 after the unstable Earl of Bothwell tried to kidnap him.

In another house in Niddry's Wynd, the final draft of the National Covenant was drawn up in 1638. This important document was a declaration against King Charles I who attempted to impose a new episcopal regime in the Church of Scotland. After being discussed by a meeting of nobles it was taken to the nearby Cowgate to be signed.

In the 18th century, Provost Edward's house became known as Lockhart's Court after a prominent legal family who lived there. Across the street lived the Erskines of Grange - a family whose story has long outlived their residence. In 1730, after twenty years of marriage, Lord Erskine and his wife Lady Grange separated. She took a house further along in Niddry's Wynd and proceeded to hound and harass her husband for his cruelty towards her. No doubt considering her a great embarrassment, Lord Erskine arranged to have Lady Grange kidnapped and removed. Imprisoned in various establishments owned by her husband's friends, the unfortunate lady was carried to the isle of St. Kilda, described as *the remotest spot of ground connected with the British Islands*. She lived there for many miserable years. When the awful truth emerged of her whereabouts, the outraged public set up a legal fund to have her returned and her husband brought to account. Alas, the help came too late. Lady Grange had been moved to the Isle of Skye, where she died in 1745.

Scandal also descended upon Niddry's Wynd in 1742, when an occupant, Martin Eccles, felt the wrath of the Edinburgh mob. Eccles

Gravestone of Lady Grange

was a surgeon - a profession treated with growing suspicion as a consequence of its unsavoury associations with the city *resurrectionists,* or bodysnatchers. These often unpleasant characters made a gruesome living by preying on the dead. The Edinburgh Medical School, much in need of fresh corpses for dissection, was none too fussy about where the bodies originated and would pay good money for suitable specimens. The bodysnatchers looked to the graveyards of the

Iron bars to prevent bodysnatching in Greyfriars cemetery

city for their supply and carried out their sinister work by dead of night. The hours were unsociable, but the money was excellent. Business thrived. Martin Eccles in Niddry's Wynd had his house and shop turned over by the mob. They were not disappointed. The body of Alexander Baxter, which had been lying peacefully in the West Kirkyard only the day before, was discovered. Eccles and some of his associates were brought in front of the magistrates and tried for being accessories to the lifting of bodies. The case was abandoned as a result of a lack of proof but Martin Eccles was hounded out of Edinburgh under a cloud of suspicion and shame.

Other notable inhabitants of Niddry's Wynd in the 18th century included the explorer James Bruce of Kinnaird, Benjamin Bell, the famous surgeon and the teacher Mr. Philp whose pupils included

St. Cecilia's Hall

Remains of Marlin's Wynd today

the poet, Robert Fergusson. The street also boasted St. Mary's Chapel, dating back to 1505 and housing the oldest authenticated Masonic Lodge in the world.

Almost all of Niddry's Wynd was destroyed to make way for the South Bridge, with one notable exception, St. Cecilia's Hall. Constructed in 1765 and named after the patron saint of music, it served the Edinburgh Musical Society and was used for concerts and recitals, including the first performance in Scotland of Handel's *Messiah*. The hall was well attended by polite Edinburgh society; amongst the regular audience were Tobias Smollett, Allan Ramsay and Daniel Defoe. During the construction of the South Bridge, the Musical Society found themselves *rendered incommodious by the taking down of the tenements at the foot of Niddry's Wynd.* The trustees of the bridge had to give an area of land in the Cowgate in recompense.

Although the exterior is much altered, St. Cecilia's Hall has been fully restored within and today houses Scotland's finest collection of early keyboard instruments.

There are sparse remnants of another ancient street, Marlin's Wynd, still in place. The top parts of the street were covered by the building of the Tron Kirk and are still visible today. Marlin, a French stonemason who came to Edinburgh in the early 16th century, has been credited with laying stone cobbles on the Royal Mile for the first time. It has been suggested in various accounts that on his death, Marlin, was actually buried beneath the street that bore his name and that the site was marked by six cobblestones in the shape of a coffin. No archaeological evidence has been found of Marlin's resting-place,

Ancient stone arches beneath the South Bridge

alas, but sections of Marlin's Wynd have come to light recently. During restoration work in the Tron Kirk, parts of the cobbled street were uncovered beneath the floor of the church. The visitor can now look down onto cellars, vaults and drainage systems. A section of stone guttering was revealed in 1997 underneath the floorboards of a house in Blair Street. Perhaps Monsieur Marlin will appear yet.

In some parts of the South Niddry Street vaults, it is still possible to make out the older sections that were incorporated into the bridge structure. In one section there are six perfectly preserved arches which were perhaps part of a medieval merchant's piazza, and now form an interior wall. In another underground room lie the remnants of a fireplace, complete with inglenook, and part of an exterior wall, nearly four feet thick. In another part of the vaults there is a sculpted stone built into a doorway that dates from the 12th century, possibly from the ruins of Holyrood Abbey. Local Edinburgh stone is of exceptional quality and can be used time and time again, as is the case here.

Enlightened Edinburgh

Edinburgh in the mid-18th century had barely expanded since its earliest days. The centre of Edinburgh consists of the Royal Mile and the Grassmarket, with a few outlying villages such as Broughton and Canonmills. The social classes lived together in the same streets, crowded on top of one another. There were no street names to be seen and people relied on the ever-present caddies to show them to their desired destination. Coal burned in open fires, simple creuzie lamps lit many homes and water was supplied through the city water wells. But the C18th was an era in which Edinburgh went through its biggest changes and developments. It was the time when David Hume and Adam Smith expounded their theories of philosophy and economics and when Scottish architects led the world in civic design. This ferment of cultural and intellectual endeavour is known as the Age of Enlightenment.

The years 1750-1800 witnessed the rise of Scotland's capital to world-class status. The largest and most ambitious of the city's projects was undoubtedly that of the New Town to be located north of the medieval city. Based on a design by the young and largely unknown architect James Craig, the gridiron structure of Princes Street, George Street and Queen Street gradually took shape in the 1760s and 1770s, and the higher echelons of society made their homes within its classical porticoes.

To prevent the Old Town being abandoned by all but the lower orders, public improvements began there also. In the heart of the Royal mile was erected the splendid neo-classical Royal Exchange which quickly attracted merchants, financiers and law officers. To the south of the city Robert Adam contributed his greatest public work, the University Quadrangle.

Although for the public good, such developments caused great disruption in the city of Edinburgh. Many old closes and wynds met their end as progress dispensed with an earlier age. It was also clear to the city developers that access to these new areas would be difficult, with the Old Town built along a steep ridge of rock sloping

The South Bridge showing the University

sharply away on each side. To drive carriages down these narrow passageways and up the other side of the hill would have been impossible. It was proposed that two bridges be built to span the valleys on either side of the Royal Mile. The North Bridge would cross the marshy trough left by the Nor' Loch and the South Bridge would span the Cowgate.

It is beneath the South Bridge that our journey will take us.

The South Bridge

These ambitious plans for the city of Edinburgh began to take shape in 1765 with the partial draining of the stinking Nor' Loch and the building of the North Bridge towards what would become the New Town. A serious setback came in 1769 when the North Bridge collapsed taking five lives. It was rebuilt on firmer foundations and reopened in 1772. The next stage of the development was a corresponding bridge to the south of the Royal Mile, first mooted in 1775. After the appointment of Trustees in 1785, the architect Robert Kay drew up a series of plans and the foundation stone was laid on 1 August of that year. The nineteen great stone arches, the three-storey buildings and the wide road running along the top were finished in less than three years, described by an observer as *an operation of astonishing celerity*. In his memoirs, Lord Cockburn remembered fondly that the only good thing about going to the High School was the excitement of crossing the partially built bridge on a set of rickety wooden planks laid down by the builders.

This astonishing feat of civic engineering was not completed without controversy. Instead of rising at a gradually sloping gradient as was intended, the Bridge is level until the University then rises up suddenly. This alteration was the result of interference by the President of the Court of Session, Robert Dundas who complained that if the original design were followed, the entrance to his house in nearby Adam Square would be below the roadway. Not only was the gentleman in question a Dundas - a family not known for submitting on matters of pride - but his half-brother, Henry Dundas, first Viscount Melville, sat on the Bridge Committee. The gradient of the slope was adjusted accordingly.

Ill-luck too, attended the opening of the South Bridge. A great ceremonial procession was planned to mark the first carriage of traffic. The city fathers decided that whoever should be the first to ride across it in a carriage would have a great honour bestowed upon them. No doubt Henry Dundas thought himself a fit candidate but the decision was taken to invite a rich, elderly woman who had lived in the area for many years. She accepted, delighted, and the preparations went ahead for the eagerly awaited day. Alas, days before the ceremony, the old lady passed away. The Bridge Committee held a meeting and agreed to honour the promise made to the lady and her family. Thus it was that one morning in March 1788, the first carriage crossed the South Bridge bearing a sombre load - the coffin of the old lady. Officially, the first person to cross the bridge was dead. Giving vent to their customary superstitions, the folk of Edinburgh took this as a terrible omen and proclaimed the bridge cursed, refusing to cross it themselves. Given the tragedy that had befallen the North Bridge only a few years earlier, their reluctance may be understandable.

In building the South Bridge many old buildings were either destroyed or altered to make way for this glorious achievement. Most of Niddry's Wynd, Peebles Wynd and what remained of Marlin's Wynd were destroyed.

On the west side of the bridge, these old streets were replaced by Hunter Square and Blair Street, named in honour of the MP and Lord Provost, James Hunter Blair, who had petitioned Parliament in support of the city improvements.

The Tron Kirk underwent major reconstruction, paid for by the Bridge Trust at a cost of £1,557. The south aisle was demolished and most of the buttresses removed. When the buildings to the east of the Kirk were taken down, it enabled local children to clamber up onto the roof and steal the lead much to the dismay of the minister. The church was considerably reduced in size by the building work but the partial demolition uncovered old coins dating back to the reigns of the English Kings Edward I and Edward II and a writing seal bearing the arms of the Arnott family from the 16th century.

As befitting a building of the new, modern age the South Bridge was designed to be practical. Eighteen of the arches were closed up on either side by shops and houses and the nineteenth was left open to allow traffic to pass through the Cowgate below. Atop the bridge were elegant buildings, purpose-built retail outlets and spacious accommodation. Beneath, the arches themselves were divided up. The resulting chambers were fitted with vaulted ceilings, fireplaces and storage areas. All those citizens who established a shop on the South Bridge found the lower, inner levels convenient for workshops, cellar space and accommodation for servants or apprentices.

Very quickly, wealthy tradesmen and high-class businesses opened shops on and around the South Bridge, invariably involving

Tron Kirk before the building of South Bridge

considerable expense. The publisher William Creech was astounded to learn that the land *on the east and the west side of it [the bridge] sold higher than perhaps ever was known in any city (even in Rome, during the most flourishing times of the Republic or Empire), to wit, at the rate of no less than £96,000 per statute acre.*

Vaults beneath the South Bridge today

The South Bridge aspired to be the great retail area of Edinburgh. The Georgian New Town was originally intended to be residential; no purpose-built shopping area had been planned or executed. The South Bridge was to fulfil this purpose. Although it was never the intention, Princes Street became commercialised very soon after construction. This did not detract from the sites on the Bridge, which attracted established, respected businesses and institutions, in addition to new hopefuls.

Within two years, there were nearly one hundred businesses operating from the South Bridge. The numbering of the buildings was unusual in that they ran consecutively down one side of the street and up the other. In 1790, most of the businesses were confined to the eastern side of the bridge and amongst them a wide variety of occupations; from drawing masters to musical instrument makers and booksellers to confectioners. The same year saw J. Gilbert, 'potter to Her Majesty' as well as the appearance in the city of the vintner, James Mather at no.20 South Bridge – a name well-known in the late 20th century amongst the revellers of Edinburgh!

In its early years of business the South Bridge attracted many booksellers, printers and publishers, largely because of its proximity to the University. Where there are writers and students, invariably, there are also public houses. One such establishment on the South Bridge was kept by Mary McKinnon, a fierce Irishwoman who would stand for no nonsense in her bar. One night whilst she was out on

View of South Bridge in the 19th c.

an errand, a group of drunken, rowdy young men entered the bar and proceeded to behave in a riotous fashion. Several young ladies were also present, behaving no less badly. On returning to her inn, Mary discovered the place in uproar and most of her furniture broken. She attempted to throw out the troublemakers but this only made matters worse and so she picked up a sharpened table knife and entered the fray. By the time order was restored, the tavern was wrecked, the regular customers had gone and William Mowat, city clerk, was slowly bleeding to death in a corner of the room. Although Mary McKinnon always proclaimed her innocence, she was tried and found guilty of his murder. She went to the gallows on 16 April 1822 and was 'hanged by the neck until dead' in front of a crowd of 20,000 people.

By 1820 over 130 businesses operated from the bridge extending from Mr. Gibson the haberdasher at no.1 to Mr. Mackay the silk dealer at no.108. There were many more booksellers and printers in the area and at no.98 were located the Goldsmiths Hall and Assay Office.

At no.83 were the premises of Andrew Melrose the celebrated grocer, tea and wine importer. This was the first retail outlet of what would become the great, world-famous Melrose Tea Company.

Niddry Street, South Niddry Street and Blair Street

By the early 19th century, businesses had appeared around the bridge in the adjoining streets. Niddry Street, South Niddry Street and Blair Street had premises which provided access to the underground vaults beneath the bridge. By examining these, a wealth of information can be found as to their use. At the top of Blair Street stood the magnificent neo-classical building that housed the King's Printers, Sir David Hunter and John Bruce Blair. The building has recently been converted into a public bar but the façade has been well preserved. Blair Street also developed into the centre of Edinburgh's rag trade with almost all the city's rag warehouses based in this street. There were several spirit dealers and two wine merchants - Falkner and Thomson at no.38, and Peter Forbes at no. 96. Several rooms within the vaults were once used for storing wine. To prevent breakage, the shelves were covered in a thick layer of sawdust upon which the wine bottles were laid, separated by small bundles of straw. For centuries the finest wines from France were shipped to the port of Leith in Edinburgh, where the city wine merchants would gather to taste samples from the wooden barrels and purchase their stock accordingly.

Wine cellars in the vaults

The Illicit Still

Whilst Messrs. Falkner, Thomson and Forbes were no doubt honest, law abiding tradesmen who paid the taxes due on the spirits they bought and sold, others were not so scrupulous. Throughout the Napoleonic Wars, the Scottish customs officials spent much of their time trying to prevent smugglers importing goods, especially wine, from France. Tradition has it that this dire situation prompted the following comment from an Edinburgh worthy, when asked how the French fleet was faring. "Like ourselves," he replied. "Confined to port!" Busy with preventing wine smuggling, the Edinburgh customs officials paid little heed to the small-scale operations of the city's illegal whisky trade. But in 1815, at the conclusion of the wars, the Customs and Excise officers turned their attentions a little closer to home. Acting on a tip-off, they raided 'certain premises' beneath the South Bridge where they discovered a large, fully operational illicit still. This had been producing gallons of illegal whisky a month, *at great injury to the revenue*. The entrepreneurs had been siphoning water from the houses above them and making the whisky below ground. To remove and sell the spirits, they had enlisted the help of an old woman, who carried out the flagons of hooch in a big green bag, muttering and cursing in such a way that people thought she was mad and kept out of her way! The distillers and their accomplice

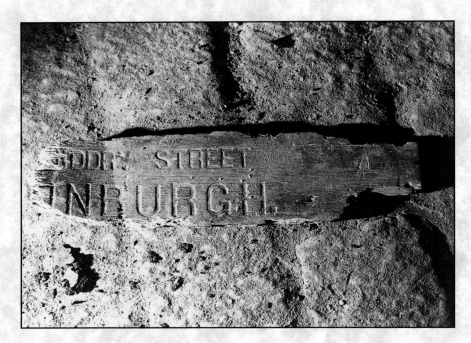

Remains of a wooden crate from the vaults

were arrested, convicted of trying to defraud the taxman and the still was completely dismantled.

Niddry Street was home to a variety of trades, but there was a predominance of leather cutters and leather merchants, some of whom may have occupied the rooms in the vaults. Sadly the street numbers of 1820 bear little resemblance to those of the present day and so it is very difficult to determine the precise locations of individual vaults.

Among the artefacts discovered in the vaults were twelve clay pots in various states of disrepair. Research has revealed that these strange objects were crucibles used for smelting metal. There were a number of businesses on or around the South Bridge in the 18th and 19th centuries that could have used such equipment, such as a brass founder, or a cutler perhaps, making knives. Although cracked and worn down, these clay crucibles have survived as a link with the people who lived and worked in the underground vaults.

Other objects have survived to increase our knowledge of how the underground vaults were used. The collections of animal bones may seem sinister but simply represent the diet of 18th century residents – sheep, cattle and even horse remains are all that is left of a family dinner 200 years ago! The many scraps of leather found may relate to a cobbler's workshop, or to a bookbinder, of which there were many in the area serving the University nearby.

Although the locality housed a thriving business quarter, many of the vaults beneath the South Bridge had to be abandoned in the ninteenth century. Despite being well planned, the Bridge had its fault in that many of the underground chambers let in water. No absorbing puddling clay had been applied, allowing moisture to drip through the stone from the road above. The effect of this can be seen today with the formation of spectacular stalactites in the vaults under South Niddry Street, the result of minerals and salt being carried down by the water.

Although many of the vaults ceased to be used as business premises in the 19th century, some of the rooms were pressed into service as air raid shelters during the Second World War. Several local residents remember that the vaults in South Niddry Street had to be pumped out as they were full of water. The underground chambers were used frequently during the war, although some people were very scared about going down into the darkness, claiming that there were 'bad spirits' at work.

Disused since the war, the vaults have since been rediscovered and opened up again for public access. Since 1997, many strange things

Crucibles found in the vaults

37

Reminders of daily life in the vaults

have been reported in the vaults beneath Niddry Street. The vaults in South Niddry Street have only recently been reopened, so there are fewer stories relating to this section.

Dripping stalactites

SINISTER STORIES from THE VAULTS

One tale of South Niddry Street dates from the 1940s and concerns a small girl called Pauline. Pauline's grandmother worked as a cleaner in a bank that once stood on the South Bridge. The little girl and her sister would often accompany the old woman to work in the evenings, helping her with her tasks. One of Pauline's regular chores was to carry large sacks of waste paper down into the vaults and empty them below. She hated doing this as she was very afraid of the dark vaults, and usually asked her sister Shelagh to help her. On one occasion, to tease her sister, Shelagh helped Pauline down into the vaults, ran back up the stairs and slammed the door behind her. Pauline hated the dark and screamed until she was released! Even more frightening however, was the long dark passageway that the girls walked passed to reach the stairs. It seemed endless, fading away into the gloom beyond.

One evening, feeling brave, the two sisters set off to investigate the corridor saying to each other that they had nothing to fear. Although a metal gate barred their way, Shelagh's bunch of keys held the key to the lock and they stepped through. Pauline shrieked with terror as the gate slammed behind her and the laughter of her sister could be heard receding up the corridor. Poor Pauline shook with fright as her eyes gradually became accustomed to her gloomy surroundings. She appeared to be in a coal cellar, a room with holes in the ceiling, piled high with sacks. The bags of

South Niddry Street vaults

fuel were stacked up around the walls and there seemed to be hunched figures sitting on top of them, holding each other in pain. Paralysed by fear, Pauline watched as the shapes moved towards her; old people, mothers with babies, small children and thin, pale men. The figures moved towards the girl, holding out their hands as if they wanted to tell her something. At last Pauline found movement in her legs and throat. She ran to the gate, screaming and yelling, beating it with her fists as the grey shapes moved closer and closer. The gate was opened and Pauline flung herself into the arms of her grandmother. As she sobbed and tried to describe what she had seen, the old woman (no stranger to these things, it would seem) comforted her and said, 'They'll no harm you, lassie, they're just poor souls trying to help you.' Although she never went back into the vaults, Pauline was to say in later years that she still shuddered with fear at the thought of the dark corridor, although she often felt sad about the poor wretches who had offered their hands in friendship.

In more recent times, tour parties have regularly been led down into the vaults. Occasionally, these groups have included someone who has claimed to have psychic abilities. The most surprising aspect of any observations made by such people is that they frequently agree down to the most minute detail with accounts related by others on a different night, perhaps months or even years apart. Visitors from around the world have described the same ghosts time and time again.

The vaults have also been the subjects of paranormal investigation, particularly by the Scottish Earth Mysteries Research Group. Part of their account runs as follows.

We entered the vaults at 11.55pm and almost immediately Catriona [an attendant psychic] sensed spirits all around her. The scene was set for a spooky two or three hours. In one room she [Catriona] felt very cold. We tried to take notes on our Dictaphone but could not get it to work... it just would not respond. Catriona complained of feeling sick. She felt this was a place of great poverty and disease and the people that lived there did not have much of a life and that things were hard for them. She sensed the workers in here had problems with their chests and lungs.

An hour had passed. Adrian noticed that one of the video cameras was not working. He then got the second of our cameras and it too was not working but having a third camera for standby, it did not bother us too much. Astonishingly, the third camera was not working. Catriona informed us that the spirits were fooling around with us and that there was nothing we could do about it.

Guides in the vaults have seen strange things

Over the last three years, the preeminent Edinburgh walking tours company, Mercat Tours, has documented a collection of unexplained sights and feelings experienced by visitors to the vaults. Each of these accounts was recorded on the day they occurred. Many of the witnesses have put their story in their own words, others have told the guide what they felt. Some of the stories come from the tour guides themselves, most of whom did not believe in ghosts before they started working in the vaults.

Several visitors have been surprised and moved by the presence of a young boy. All those who have experienced him have said that he is very young, about 5 years old. Several people have suggested that his name is Jack/James or Henry, and all agree that he is a lively, cheeky wee boy. James seems to be a bit of an attention seeker and has been known to pull on people's clothing, or even tug on their hair! Here is a small selection of sightings of James.

Emma saw the ghost of a wee boy running around. She was laughing and looking around her because apparently he was zooming all over the place and running round her legs. She thought that he was a boy of between four and six years old. He is not an unhappy spirit; he is having an adventure. He likes seeing all the people...and thinks, because he is so young, that we are all really funny.

> -Emma Cairns is an Australian psychic who visited the vaults in 1998 accompanied by two tour guides, one of whom wrote the report quoted here.

When I was in the cobbler's room I saw the ghost of a boy.
-A young girl on the tour, who also described the boy to the guide.

I felt a strange cold hand grip my hand.... I thought it was my mum but she had gloves on. It was very weird because I heard a little voice laughing playfully.... I think he wanted to play with me. Strange!
-Ashley, Edinburgh

A lady felt compelled to remove her hand from her pocket and as it was hanging by her side she was clenching and unclenching it, grasping something.... she was sure it was a little boy, trying to hold her hand for comfort.
-Bob [tour guide]

In one room, I saw a small, pale figure, pale hair and face, wearing dark clothes. It was just standing there watching the group.
-Amber Rosin, Australia

I looked down toward the darkened corridor and saw a figure slide into view. The figure was only about 3 and a half to 4 feet tall, with blonde hair and pale skin. He appeared to have a high collar with dark clothing... he appeared to move slightly and look around the crowd. I then grabbed my girlfriend's hand and pointed the figure out. She saw it too.
-Steve Hogney, Australia

While in the final room (double-vaulted) I had walked into the room and felt like I had sensed something in the very far corner.... my friend said: "It looks as if there is a small boy with a ball".... I concentrated, and we got his name... It was 'Henry'.
-Two tourists

A child's shoe in the vaults

A young American girl (on the same tour as opposite) *saw the little boy in the corner of the last room. She said that he had a ball under his left arm and that she had felt he wanted a friend. She felt the little boy hold her hand. She thought his name was Henry.... Incidentally, I did not mention the ghost of the little boy on this tour.*

-Frances [tour guide]

Other strange experiences in the vaults seem to be connected to a male character – a man who is most unhappy at having his territory invaded. Some unsuspecting visitors have felt a hot breath on their face, or heard a gruff voice telling them to leave quickly. Some people claim to have been pushed and shoved. Here are some of their accounts.

Emma told us [tour guides] *to wait behind her. She stood there for a minute or two looking ahead of her. Then she suddenly stumbled backwards. Later she told us of the presence of malevolent male ghost who was very strong.... He had told her to get out of the vaults, and she had tried to reason with him, saying she respected that this was his territory.... he then made a lunge at her (which is when we saw her stumble backwards), and she saw him very clearly. She described him as a big man, wearing a filthy blue overcoat and carrying something jagged in his hand – a knife, perhaps, or a broken bottle. He said, "Get out!" repeatedly. He was very territorial.*

-Emma Cairns, from the guide's report

One middle-aged American lady was convinced we had a 'plant', i.e. somebody put there to jump out and scare people. She said that somebody was breathing on her face with hot, stinking breath. When she came out of that room her glasses were all steamed up. She also said that simultaneously something was tugging at the bottom of her coat, like a child might do.

-Fran [tour guide]

When I walked into the room I heard a deep grunt or breath. It sounded as though the person was really fed up.

-James Bowb, Surrey

I was in the wine vaults, telling the story of a man breathing on people, when a loud, male voice moaned.... I resumed the story.... I was interrupted again by the same sound. I asked if anyone in the group had made the noise, but they were just as scared as me. No-one would own up to it, and they had all heard it.... Gordon [another guide] *later told me that he had had a similar experience some days earlier.*

-Bram [tour guide]

The white room.... I couldn't go in. In the corridor there was a presence against the wall, an oppressive one. I couldn't see anything, but it was a strange sensation. Closest thing would be like someone breathing on you.

-Renee, Edinburgh

In the double vaulted room I saw a man wearing a tri-corner hat, white ruff and leather boots, leaning against the far wall"

-Dennis, Edinburgh

In the double room.... I saw the same man Dennis saw: sharp features, wearing a hat. I thought I was imagining it and looked away, and when I felt tempted to look again, he was still there.

-Janie McBrierty, Edinburgh

In recent times the large room has been the most disturbing room in the vaults. It was here, with a group of ten, that I saw a complete figure of a man. I find it difficult to write down the details as I was frankly very scared indeed. I saw him over the heads of the visitors. He was standing in the doorway leading to the back corridor, looking into the small room on the right as you look back. He turned his head and smiled at me! I realise just how bizarre this all sounds, but even if it was just my imagination, it was very real at the time. He was tall, strong looking, with dark hair and knee-high boots. His eyes were only dark hollows. It took a lot of effort and concentration for me to go back to the vaults again.

-Gordon [tour guide]

Remnants in the vaults

Footsteps have often been heard in the vaults. Could it be the same character?

I had 13 people on the tour. We were followed by footsteps most of the way through the vaults. 4 people heard them.

-Fran [tour guide]

In the second from last vault I heard noises, possibly footsteps, coming from where we had already been.

-June, Edinburgh

My boyfriend and I.... heard the squeaking of shoes in the small 'very haunted' room.

-Melinda Welton, Australia

I was in the white room telling a story. I'd switched the lights out, so I couldn't see a thing.... I suddenly began to hear a sort of squeak I can't explain it! It sounded like the squeaking of shoes on my left-hand side. I switched the light on and I could still hear the squeaking, so I was trying to look at everyone's feet. The next night, I heard the same thing again. I hadn't turned out the light, I could see everyone clearly, and I could hear this squeaking sound coming from the right. Everyone in my group was looking at the girl we thought was making the noise but she swears she wasn't doing anything....

-Jane [tour guide]

I definitely heard footsteps.

-Stephanie Hammond, Edinburgh

All through the story I was completely conscious of the squeaking boots. It wasn't the sound I imagined. It's a very deep sound and I knew it wasn't coming from the area the group was standing in. At the end of the story I asked if anyone had heard anything. Two girls spoke at the same time; one said "footsteps", the other said, "squeaking".

-Karen [tour guide]

Three people distinctly heard footsteps in the corridor, not upstairs, but right next to us. One girl was convinced someone was about to jump out. She saw the boots and described them vividly; black, shiny and knee-length.

-Calum [tour guide]

There is one room in the vaults, now no longer open to visitors that served as a workshop in times past. As a consequence of leather scraps found in this room, it has been assumed that the room was used by a worker of leather or perhaps a shoemaker. Here are just a handful of reports of sightings in this room.

A man stands, barefoot, in a leather apron, in the glare of the light. He is happy to see all the people, but cannot understand why he has no work to do. He wants us to clean up the mess – it's getting in his way.

-Ebhlin McIntosh, a psychic from the U.S., as reported to a tour guide.

He is a small man...and is wearing a white shirt with the sleeves rolled up and a leather apron around his waist. He is well aware of the groups coming round and is quite happy that they do so. He would like it if everyone said hello and goodbye to him.

-Emma Cairns

Debbie saw and described the cobbler quite clearly. A small man, standing at a workbench.

-Debbie, a psychic from London, as reported by a tour guide

I saw a figure against the wall crouching, as though sitting on a foot-high stool. It was a man who appeared to have his elbows on his knees. He looked to be working on something. He twisted his head and looked up slightly, appearing to look towards me.

-Steve Hogney, Australia

The cobbler was described to me tonight. A small man, wearing a white shirt, bald and with an apron. The girl who described him said there was a feeling of happiness in the cobbler's room.

-Calum [tour guide]

(The cobbler) *is 50-ish, quite short but stocky, wearing a long leather apron. He is happy to see us, but wishes that we would stay longer.*

-American visitor

In the first room in the vaults I saw a man about 35-45 years old sitting on a pile of stone plates, watching Jill (the guide). *He didn't seem angry, so I tried to talk to him just with my mind. I told him I hoped he didn't mind all these tours, but he had gotten used to them anyway.*

-Andrew, Australia

This room has also caused some distress to visitors. This is what has been reported.

There is a woman wearing a black veil. She is unhappy about our presence.

-Ebhlin McIntosh

The negative thing about that room is the ghost of the woman to the right of the doorway, wearing a veil. She is very angry and distressed about something and does not wish to communicate.... Of all the ghosts in the vaults she is potentially the most powerful, but she is confined to a small area. As long as people don't stand in that corner there should be no trouble.

-Emma Cairns

The woman in black was angry because of an indiscretion by her husband, so she feels animosity to women who are pregnant.

-Nicolle, a psychic

In the far right-hand corner she saw a woman with a very unpleasant presence to her. She appears deranged and she was scratching furiously at her chest.

-Debbie

Someone on my tour was pushed away from the wall. She was pregnant, which confirms what some psychics have said about the presence in that corner.

-Frances [tour guide]

I was describing what a positive room it was, and this woman said to me later that she hated it, that it made her very uneasy. Guess where she was standing? I hasten to add that I had said nothing about the veiled woman in the corner until she picked up on it.

-Calum [tour guide]

A horse skull found in the vaults

A pregnant woman standing in the 'veiled presence' corner, underneath the red light, became very distressed and asked to be taken out of the vaults. I took her and her husband up on to Niddry Street, whereupon she apologised. She explained that when she had stood in the corner, she had felt a fist pressing into the small of her back, and had an overwhelming compulsion to get out of the room. She assured me that she was not usually a nervy person, and that she loved ghost stories, but that she had been genuinely frightened in the vaults.

-Cathleen [tour guide]

Can animals come back as spirits? What do you make of the following reports?

There was a good fire going [in the caretaker's room]. The man has a dog that stays with him in the vaults.

-Ebhlin McIntosh

In the caretaker's room I felt a dog brush against the side of my leg. It felt shaggy and happy.

-Joanne Carlow

I set my eyes on the corridor, and saw a little terrier peeping around the doorway. It was a kind of tan or brown colour, with wiry, longish hair. I couldn't see its tail. Ten minutes later, Fran told us about the guard's dog....

-A young girl from London

A woman told me that there was a dog in the vaults. (I never mention the dog on my tour.) I said, "What makes you say that?" She said "Oh! I just heard a dog bark." I asked her if she had seen it. She hadn't actually seen it, but she said it was a small brown and white terrier, possibly female.

-Frances [tour guide]

In the very first room I felt a warm fur feeling round the bottom of my leg. The same thing happened in every room.

-Jane Smith, England

Another young girl was sure she saw a hawk-like bird above us in the corridor.

-Calum [tour guide]

On a tour of mine, a woman became hysterical in the double-vaulted room, as she claimed a bat or a bird was flapping in her face. She was very, very distressed.

-Gordon [tour guide]

In the double vaulted room, a woman felt that something black was going to swoop down from the gap in the ceiling. She was absolutely terrified, especially when I told her the stories of previous similar experiences.

-Frances [tour guide]

48

Occasionally it happens that somebody does not actually see anything, but they just experience a strange feeling.

I felt it was like a wall that was making it difficult to walk through the corridor. Once on the other side of the corridor I felt much more relaxed, but until that point it was an incredibly intense feeling.
-Renee, Edinburgh

One man would not enter the room, he said there was something 'like a wall' over the entrance.
-Bram [tour guide]

Not a nice place. The feelings that I get there are horrible. I no longer enter that room. On one tour, a woman burst into tears inside the room, but claimed she did not know why. On leaving she was very distressed.
-Gordon [tour guide]

A man tried to take a photograph in the white room (twice) but his camera wouldn't work, even though he took photos with no trouble in other parts of the vaults and on the Royal Mile.
-Cathleen [tour guide]

A face has appeared in the wall at the back of the room, directly facing the door. It appears mask-like and is only a foot or so off the floor. Now reported twice on my tours. The anxiety of visitors is generally heightened here.
-Gordon [tour guide]

The sensation I felt was as if someone had gripped my leg just below the knee.... I was extremely cold and started to feel uncomfortable....
-visitor from the U.S.A.

One lady started to get very agitated and had to be taken out. She was very pale and shaky and got awfully disoriented on the way out. She told me that she couldn't bear it down there and that she had been really frightened. She was adamant that there was an evil presence.
-Fran [tour guide]

Although most of the rooms in the vaults were used as storage or workshops, it has been suggested that they had other, less innocent uses. The Edinburgh branch of the Hellfire Club held its meetings beneath the South Bridge and several brothels were reported in the area. The exact sites are, alas, unknown.

In the back room [a tourist] heard the low murmuring of 14 or 15 people. She asked if it had been used as a prison at one time.
-Judith [tour guide]

[In the double vaulted room] *one man (who claimed to be psychic) said: "Was there a pub in here?" He said he could sense benches along the walls, and dirty, smelly drunk people.*

-Fran [tour guide]

The back room felt like a pub or a brothel.

-Emma Cairns

As you can see from the accounts above, the underground vaults have been the location for several apparently ghostly happenings. Many visitors to the vaults were in no doubt that they felt or saw a spiritual presence while others have admitted that the underground vaults have a strange atmosphere. Whether you are a believer in the supernatural or not, this part of Edinburgh provides a fascinating glimpse into the city's past. Wandering through the 18th century chambers, many disused for nearly two centuries, the visitor can experience living and working conditions of times past. And perhaps, as has happened on so many occasions, you may be lucky, or unlucky enough to experience the supernatural for yourself. Either way, the underground vaulted chambers are not to be missed.

The city of Edinburgh has a rich and often gruesome history that stretches back hundreds of years. Every close and wynd seems to have a story hidden within involving witchcraft, hauntings or foul deeds. These dark tales have fascinated people for centuries and their power to intrigue has not diminished with the passing years. Indeed, interest in the more sinister side of Edinburgh's past seems to grow and grow. In recent times there has been much rumour and speculation about underground Edinburgh. Tours to the subterranean parts of the city have satisfied the curiosity of thousands of visitors and local people. Many people descend every year to see the rooms where the plague victims perished or the dark and gloomy vaults where folk lived and worked over two centuries ago.

Whilst this book has given you an insight into these atmospheric chambers, the thrill of viewing them in person simply cannot be reproduced. Mercat Tours operates visits to Edinburgh's hidden underground every day, providing visitors with an entertaining and historically accurate look at Edinburgh's hidden past. No gimmicks or special effects are used. All accounts contained within this book have been faithfully recorded from the experiences of the tour guides and the visitors themselves. We cannot guarantee a ghost, but we can tell you what many others have seen, heard and felt. Dare you join us?